TIPS FOR TRAVELING SALESMEN

By

HERBERT N. CASSON

B. C. FORBES PUBLISHING CO.
120 Fifth Avenue New York City

Kessinger Publishing's Rare Reprints
Thousands of Scarce and Hard-to-Find Books!

- • • •
- • • •
- • • •
- • • •
- • • •
- • • •
- • • •
- • • •
- • • •
- • • •
- • • •
- • • •
- • • •
- • • •
- • • •
- • • •
- • • •
- • • •

We kindly invite you to view our extensive catalog list at:
http://www.kessinger.net

PREFACE

THIS book is, I believe, the first one of its kind for traveling salesmen. Scores of books have been written, in a general way, about salesmanship; but none has been written directly for the salesman on the road.

The work of a traveling salesman is entirely different from the work of any one else. The goodwill of a concern, as well as the profits, depends mainly upon the skill of the traveling salesman.

In fact, the function of the traveling salesman has never yet been fully appreciated. He is usually treated as a mere carrier of samples, whereas he is no such thing. He is the business-getter and goodwill builder of his house or corporation. He is a creator of new business and a conserver of what has already been done.

To know his goods is only the A.B.C. of a traveling salesman's technique. He must know human nature, too, and how to deal with all sorts and conditions of men.

No one, I venture to say, can be too wise or too competent for the position of traveling salesman; and most of us who have been on the road have fallen far short of our possibilities.

This book is offered, therefore, to all sales managers and traveling salesmen in the hope that it may enable them to sell more goods more easily and pleasantly.

THE AUTHOR

CONTENTS

I

BEGIN BY TALKING HIM

CHAPTER I

BEGIN BY TALKING HIM

Learn Your Customers' Hobbies, Personal Likes and Dislikes — Base Your Approach on These — Then Show Goods

THE first commandment of traveling salesmen is: " Thou shalt not enter as an unwelcome intruder."

A salesman is not at all like a shop assistant — no such luck. A shop assistant stays in the shop and waits on customers who want to buy; whereas a salesman goes about and tries to sell goods to people who never sent for him.

The salesman enters uninvited. He tries to see a busy man with whom he has no appointment. He is always butting in — forcing himself and his goods upon the attention of people who are thinking of something else.

In the whole world of trade and commerce probably no one has so hard and baffling a job as a traveling salesman. He has to deal with other people, over whom he has no authority. He has to depend absolutely upon his own skill, likeableness, quickness and information. He has a little routine work — mere order-taking. But if he depends on this, he will soon find himself out of a job.

So, as you can see, much depends on how he begins, how he enters a place. The first half-minute may make him or break him.

He can't go in boldly and say: " Well, here I am again. You can't put me out. I have a legal right to come in and I want an order. I must have it, in fact, as I am paid on commission." That entry would be effective, no doubt, on the stage; but it wouldn't do in real life. Neither should a salesman come in timidly and present his card, " I represent Jones and Brown," etc.

All young salesmen start off in that way and find, after a while, that a card carries you nowhere.

No. There is one best way to enter a place and it is remarkable how many travelers are not aware of it.

Every call must be PERSONAL — that is the first rule in salesmanship.

You must prepare before you go in. You must decide beforehand what you are going to do and say. You must be active, not passive; and you must treat every man differently, according to his nature.

Once a big firm trained its travelers to memorize a selling talk. They all said the same thing to everybody. This experiment proved to be a complete failure. It changed the salesmen into poll-parrots. Of course, they failed.

No two dealers are alike, and in the beginning of the sale (not the closing) you must treat each man in a personal way.

You must ask yourself, What is he thinking about? What are his fears — his hopes — his troubles? You must fit into his present line of thought.

One good way to begin your sales talk is to remind him of something he said to you on your last visit. If you have a good memory, you can recall something he said or did. If not, you can make a habit of putting down sayings or events in your notebook.

It is a good plan for every salesman to keep a Card List of his customers, and to put down on these cards any sayings and actions that are worth remembering. Some travelers go as far as to put down on these cards all the fads, beliefs, sports, and so forth of their customers.

On one card, for instance, he may write: " Fond of fishing. Owns a Scotch collie. Goes to the horse races."

On another card he may write: " Keeps a Jersey cow and White Leghorn hens. Has won prizes for hens."

In a word, it is wise to approach a man on the side of his hobbies, rather than his business. He is always more human and accessible on the hobby side.

Then, as soon as you begin to talk business, put something interesting into his hand — something new and special out of your samples.

Sell to his eyes rather than to his ears. Few men are good listeners. While you are talking, their minds are thinking of something else. How can you prevent this? How can you get a man's concentrated attention? By putting something interesting in his hands.

The optic nerve is twenty-two times stronger than the nerve that leads from the ear to the brain. Hence, it follows that what a man SEES has a stronger influence upon him than what he HEARS.

If you will call up in your mind a play that you saw several years ago you will find that you remember the most striking scenes, but not the words.

That is why we must always appeal more to the eye than the ear. And when a customer is holding one of your samples and you are pointing out its qualities you are appealing to *both* eye and ear, and the sense of touch as well. Once you have got as far as this, the worst is over. You will probably get an order. You have won his favorable attention, and unless he is suddenly called away or interrupted he will be likely to buy your goods.

The next point to aim at is the size of the

order. He wants the goods, but the query is: How much?

The customer's mind is now shifting from the goods to the probability of selling them — can he sell a dozen or can he sell four dozen? He is now thinking on right lines and a wise salesman will be quick to think *with* him, instead of showing him other goods, or pointing out the qualities of the goods.

The question now is: What is the possible market for these goods?

If the salesman can say that Blank and Company in Boston sold three dozen in a week, that will be a help.

If he can say that his firm is spending $100,000 advertising these goods in national newspapers and magazines, that, too, will be a help.

If he can say that seventeen firms have re-ordered the goods during the past week, or mention any other fact that will prove the salability of the goods, he will increase the size of his order.

Too many small orders are taken. Of that

there is no doubt. And the reason is that the salesman did not convince the dealer that the goods were quick sellers.

If the salesman can go further than this and suggest window displays, or advertisements, or any special demonstration, this, also, will help to make his order larger.

The point to remember is that as soon as the customer is interested in the goods, you must talk from His point of view. Talk as a partner. Don't talk about BUYING. Talk about SELLING to the public.

This wipes out all antagonism between you and the customer. It enables you both to aim at one result — the sale of a larger quantity of goods.

You are talking HIM, not your goods — not your firm — not yourself.

A certain salesman of insurance, who sells $2,000,000 of insurance a year, follows out this plan to a remarkable degree.

Before he approaches a man, he learns as much as possible about the man's business, health, family, ambitions, temperament, etc

Then he prepares a plan of insurance that will best suit this man. He works out the man's point of view. Then, not before, he goes to him and says: " How would you like to have a plan of insurance like this? "

If a man has two sons at school, for instance, this salesman says to him: " How would you like to be sure, in case you die next week, that your two sons would have enough money to complete their education, and $5,000 apiece when they are 21? "

As you see, he talks HIM. He compels attention. He almost compels the sale of a policy. He is almost irresistible, because he comes to the prospect from the prospect's point of view.

He treats his customer as a CLIENT, not merely as a Buyer. He does it sincerely. He does not try to over-sell.

If you go into a small shop, begin by BUYING something. Why not? It will be a dollar well spent. If you go into a large shop, begin by appreciating the goods now on sale, or the window display.

Don't come charging down on a man as a salesman.

Don't make him put his hands up and prepare for a fight.

Don't thrust YOUR point of view on him. Don't attack. Don't coerce. Don't launch a selling talk at him as if you were trying to torpedo him into giving you an order.

Your customer is not an enemy. His interests are, in the long run, the same as yours. He is your partner, your friend. You are a fellow-salesman and you are both interested in selling more and more goods to the public.

BEGIN BY TALKING HIM.

II

USE MORE EAR AND LESS TONGUE

CHAPTER II

USE MORE EAR AND LESS TONGUE

Give Your Customer the Center of the Stage — The Main Thing Is Not to Talk, but to Sell

A TRAVELING salesman is not a lecturer and a customer is not an audience. There is a fact that will greatly increase the selling efficiency of any salesman who is clever enough to see the force of it.

Too much talk! That's what kills customers. Many a manufacturer might have a cemetery at the back of his factory. And on most of the gravestones you would see this epitaph:

" Sacred to the memory of J. B. Jones, Inc., — formerly a customer, but talked to death by one of our travelers."

Most travelers fancy that they are paid to talk. They are not. They are paid to SELL — quite a different thing.

They drown their customers in a flood of talk; and then go to bed without a guilty conscience.

Talk! Argue! Prove! That is their idea of salesmanship, and it is quite wrong. I am pointing out a better way: Listen! Agree! Serve!

In a shop, once, I heard a traveling salesman say to the storekeeper: " You can't deny that, can you? "

Such a man, you see, was entirely misplaced as a salesman. He should have been a Policeman or a Night-watchman.

Isn't it true that most salesmen have the wrong idea of a customer? Their ideal customer is one who listens mutely, and at every pause says, " Send me three dozen." A sort of tongue-tied, easily persuaded man with an inexhaustible bank account — he is their ideal of a perfect customer.

Maybe he would be, but — there are very few such men. Most customers would sooner talk than listen and they abhor writing checks above all things.

The fact is that a salesman ought to encourage the customer to talk. The more the customer talks, at first, the better. A man is like a barrel — you must empty him before you can fill him.

A wise salesman will draw his customer out. He will ask questions — all manner of questions.

If he happens in the shop before the holidays, he will ask the customer where he is going this Summer. And if he happens in after the holidays, he will ask the customer if he has had a pleasant vacation.

He will, in a word, give the customer the center of the stage. He — the salesman — will become the audience.

This is not what the customer expects. It is a welcome change. It gives the salesman a running start.

A salesman should ask his customer questions for two reasons:

1. In order to win the favorable attention and goodwill of the customer.

2. In order to learn the opinions of the cus-

tomer about the goods and the preferences of the public.

One of a salesman's duties is to keep his concern in touch with the customers and the public. If he does this well, he can almost double his value to his employer. He can, eventually, become the sales manager if he learns how to suit the public.

A salesman must be a learner, as well as a teacher. He must avoid that air of superiority that some salesmen possess. He must not be a Know-it-all. And he must suppress the natural tendency that most men have to show off.

A really skilled and ripened salesman will draw out the knowledge of his customer. He will play second fiddle in the conversation, with an eye single to a big order. Very few salesmen — perhaps not one in a hundred — can reach this point of skill and self-control; but it is well worth reaching.

From the point of view of psychology, too, there is a good reason for encouraging the customer to talk.

Most merchants are in a state of suppressed

irritation or discouragement. They cannot often talk freely to their own customers. They bottle up their discontent. This makes them abnormal — perhaps morbid or irascible.

It certainly prevents them from buying goods.

Consequently, one of the first steps in the process of selling is to let the customer give free vent to his suppressed fears and complaints.

Talking about his own difficulties normalizes him. That is what we learn from Freud, of Vienna.

Get the poison out — that is how to restore a man to normalcy. Let him talk. Let him talk himself into a better humor and a better attitude towards the world. Then, when he cracks a joke and lights his cigar, the time has come to sell him goods.

As you can see, this is revolutionary. It is not taught by the professors of salesmanship, nor in the courses of study. It is new. It is precisely the opposite of what most traveling salesmen do, especially the younger ones.

The sales talk, that we hear so much about, is not indispensable.

The thrusting, forceful, dominating, spell-binding salesman is a crude specimen, and only fitted to sell to crude people.

A first-class salesman need not even be a good conversationalist. He may be a poor talker — not glib at all; and he may send in twice as many orders as the glibbest man in his firm.

Nearly all our books and courses on Salesmanship have been putting the emphasis on the wrong place. The main thing is not to talk, but to SELL.

So, if more goods can be sold by listening than by talking, then we must listen. We must put a check on the ready tongue and we must use the reluctant ear.

Few men are silent and taciturn. Certainly, few merchants are. Nine out of ten enjoy talking about their own affairs with a friendly outsider. A man can say to a visitor many things that he will not like to admit to his fellow-citizens.

A wise, sympathetic salesman, as a listener, is a boon to many a merchant, who is compelled to put on a bold front to his own family, employees and fellow-citizens.

A safe and sensible man, to whom one can talk freely, is often a godsend to a merchant who has suppressed his complaints to the point of explosion.

A salesman should listen to the flow of pent-up troubles, not because it is his professional duty to do so, but because as a salesman he is interested in people and their affairs.

A salesman is not like an engineer, a draughtsman, an inventor, a designer. He must not have a great power of concentration, as these men have.

Few people can listen courteously, instead of impatiently, or formally. Most people ENDURE rather than listen. They listen because they must, not because they take a pleasure in listening.

But you may have noticed that the most popular man in any club is the one who is the best listener. He is the one who will have the largest funeral, you may be sure of that.

On the other hand, the man who is the bore of any club is the man who insists upon doing most of the talking. He is the room-emptier, the chaser.

One definition of a bore is: A man who keeps on talking about himself when you want to talk about yourself — a very correct definition.

This definition would include the average traveling salesman, as his main idea is to monopolize the talking, and to talk about his concern and his goods.

To bore a customer — how does that help to sell goods? Of what use is it to talk to a man who is thinking of something else? And of what use is it to show samples to a man who is regarding you as a nuisance?

None. The actual process of selling should not begin until you have secured the favorable interest of the customer, and this you do by talking HIM and by listening to him.

No jockey makes his horse do its utmost at

the start; and neither will any competent sales-man try to sell goods at the start.

On the contrary, he will do his best to efface himself and to bring his customer to the front, at first.

He will remember that wise saying, " Blessed are the meek, for they shall inherit the earth."

He will remember that courtesy always comes first, and that courtesy consists of a sympathetic interest in the affairs of others.

He will meet every customer as man to man, or friend to friend, before they become seller and buyer. It pays — and it's right.

III

PUT SERVICE BEFORE SAMPLES

CHAPTER III

PUT SERVICE BEFORE SAMPLES

*Study Your Customer's Problems and Needs
— Try to Help Him to Move His Goods*

EVERY traveling salesman carries samples, but how many carry service? Possibly not one out of fifty — not 2 per cent.

The man who carries service is exceptional. He stands high. He stands at the top of his profession. He is the latest and highest type of salesman.

Long ago, when business was greedier than it is to-day, a salesman's motto was: " Study my own pocket."

Then he grew wiser. He found greediness didn't pay, and he learned a new motto — " Study my goods."

Recently a few salesmen — not many — have gone further still. They have formed a

27

still better motto: "STUDY MY CUSTOMER'S PROBLEMS."

This is the highest point of salesmanship, and very few ever reach it.

After you have listened to your customer's talk — after you have had a personal opening, then you settle down to business and show him how to re-sell your goods.

Almost invariably a retailer needs help or advice. Few retailers know as much about their own business as they should.

The retailer does not want any more dead stock. He has a dread of skilled salesmen who over-sell him. The burnt child dreads the fire; and he has often been burnt.

He is a worried, flurried, hurried man. He is not thinking about you and your goods. He is thinking about bad debts and old stock, and bills payable, and his wife's disposition, and his competitors.

So, when you go into a shop, don't march up with a stiff tread, like a sheriff, and plague the poor shopkeeper with your demands for his personal attention.

Go and look at his stock. See what he

lacks. Study out his stock situation. Then go and talk to him about it, when he is ready to talk business.

Do try to get it into your mind that the shopkeeper has not been lying awake nights, waiting for the glorious arrival of yourself and your wonderful samples. He has not. He does not regard your samples as a rival show to the Follies. He wouldn't pay a penny admission to see all you've got. So, you must shift your point of view from Samples to Service.

As soon as you go into a shop don't idle about and wait to see your customer. Get busy. Act like a new employee. Act like a worthwhile son-in-law. Help to dress one of the windows. Talk to the shop assistants. Find out the shop news. Show them a new method of display. Take a friendly, practical interest in getting the goods sold to the public.

Be active, not passive. Be positive, not negative. Lend a hand. Give a half-hour's actual service. Then bring on your samples.

A traveling salesman, in fact, must have a

larger idea of himself and his job. He is not merely an order-taker. Neither is he merely a salemaker. A better word for him would be a distributor.

He sells to people who sell again — that is the point to remember at the moment.

His aim is not merely to put more goods on a retailer's shelves, if he is a wise, far-sighted salesman, doing his best to make permanent patrons.

His aim is rather to help the retailer to sell the goods to the public. He is not really selling To the retailer, but THROUGH him, to the consumers.

When a retailer buys goods, they are only HALF sold. They must be re-sold to their final owners.

There are two steps in a sale, or three. When a manufacturer sells to a wholesaler, who sells to a retailer, who sells to the public, there are three steps in the sale.

If the goods remain unsold on the shelves of the retailer, the salesman who sold them is less likely to receive another order.

So, a salesman does not say to a retailer: "I want to sell you some goods." No. He says: "I want you to sell some goods"—a vastly different thing.

As soon as he works from this point of view he becomes the retailer's best friend. The retailer is no longer afraid of him. He has made the retailer a client, not merely a customer.

This new point of view will be accepted only by the ablest and most intelligent salesmen. The others will say: "Am I my brother's keeper?" They will be afraid that this means more work.

They will say: "It is none of my business whether a retailer sells his stock or not."

The average salesman may not see that when he helps the retailer he helps himself as well. The best way to make retailers buy more is to help them to sell more. That is a fact that cannot be denied.

Let us carry the subject up a bit higher. Let us think about TURNOVER. Few travelers do.

Turnover means how quickly a retailer sells his goods. A jeweler, for instance, turns over his goods once a year, while a grocer turns over his goods about twelve times a year.

Butchers and greengrocers and florists and dairies have a quick turnover. A newsboy has the quickest turnover of all, as he sells out his stock twice a day — morning and evening.

The quicker the turnover, the less capital you need to do a certain amount of business.

A retailer can practically double his capital, without borrowing or investing, if he doubles his turnover.

Goods that sell slowly are the bane of all retailers. They tie capital up. They pull down profits. They often wipe out profits altogether.

There you have the reasons for Special Sales — goods that stick. When a wise retailer finds that he cannot sell a certain line of goods at a profit, he sells them at cost so as to get his money back. But that sort of an adventure makes no profit for anyone.

There are too many cut-price sales — all retailers know that. Far too much merchandise is sold at a loss. It was either wrongly bought or badly sold. The blame lay somewhere between the salesmen and the retailer; and an efficient traveler, instead of trying to dodge the blame, will freely shoulder his share of it. He will do all he can to help the retailer to re-sell.

A traveler, you see, is a professional salesman. He is a specialist on sales. He does nothing else but sell.

A retailer, on the contrary, has to do all sorts of things. He has to be a financier, an employer, an owner of buildings and motorcars and merchandise.

A retailer usually has so many miscellaneous worries that he does not pay enough attention to salesmanship and window display. He has so much routine work that he neglects special sales efforts.

A salesman, consequently, can show him how to dress his windows more effectively. He can tell him what certain New York merchants are doing.

He can show him several ways of pushing dead goods, such as putting them on a table ten feet from the front door, or having the cleverest salesgirl give a demonstration, or making a special offer to sell on instalments.

He may even go further than this and show him how to collect his slow accounts. No one knows how to do this perfectly, but a retailer usually does it very awkwardly.

The problem is how to write a sharp but tactful letter that will bring in the money without offending the customer.

A salesman should have some samples of such letters in his pockets — letters that have been tried by other firms with good results.

I once met one wise salesman who helps retailers with their Income Tax perplexities. Many retailers are paying more than the law requires, as tax collectors have no conscience in these matters. So, this salesman had studied the law carefully, and he could tell a retailer of all the rebates or exemptions that are legal.

As you may imagine, a salesman who can save a retailer $200 taxes a year will not depend upon his samples for his orders.

In such ways as these, and many others, a

traveling salesman may become a wise coun-
selor to his retailers.

He sincerely concerns himself with any matter that promotes the welfare of his customers
— that is the point.

" But," a Sales Manager may say, " all this
takes time. How can a traveler cover his territory if he treats customers as clients and
partners? "

The answer is: The size of the orders is more
important than the number of visits. A traveling salesman is too often regarded as a mere
postman — a mere legger — dashing quickly
from door to door and collecting the greatest
possible number of refusals.

It is better to make one sale in 40 minutes
than it is to be given four refusals in an hour.
Four times nothing is nothing.

When I was a lad in a retail shop, in the early
'80s, in a remote village in Canada, the coming
of a traveling salesman was a great event. He
remained in the village a day and that day
was one of the few shining days of the year.

Always, he entertained us. He told us the

stories and gossip of the big world, which we had never seen.

He was full of fun, wisdom, news, ideas, personal talk. In the evening, we all gathered in the little hotel and listened to him until 10 o'clock, when all good villagers went to bed.

That man was my ideal traveling salesman and is still. Why should his type be abolished? Why should we now have bloodless clerks as travelers, thrusting their unwelcome cards and samples into the faces of retailers and dashing for the next train?

Why can we not restore the profession of traveling salesman to its former height of sociability and service? Any firm that dares to do this will double its sales in two years.

Once, when I was 14, a traveler showed me the one right way to wrap a parcel — pressing the paper towards the edges — making tight corners instead of baggy ones.

Another traveler showed me the conjurer's art of putting a coin on my hand, head up, and turning it upside down on the counter, still with the head up. What boy would ever forget such things?

All this was putting Service before Samples. It was selling goods in a friendly, helpful, human way. It was EFFICIENT SALESMANSHIP, of a kind that is now rare in these days of big organizations.

We should lose no time in getting back to it.

IV

MENTION QUALITY BEFORE PRICE

CHAPTER IV

MENTION QUALITY BEFORE PRICE

You Must Know Your Goods Through and Through — Art of Dramatizing a Sale

THOUSANDS of sales are lost every year — perhaps hundreds of thousands — because the salesman mentions price first.

These price tellers! They are in almost every retail shop. They are everywhere. You will even find them — dozens of them — in the ranks of traveling salesmen.

You will find it a rule that if a salesman at once tells you the price of an article, it is a sign he knows nothing about the article itself.

And what could possibly be more foolish than to hurl the price at a customer before he has time to see the value of the goods?

Why tell him what he must PAY, before you show him what he will GET?

Why make haste to tell him what he will Lose, before he knows what he will Gain?

The real professional rule, as every skilled salesman knows, is: Never mention price until the customer thinks it is more.

If the customer at once asks the price, do not tell him. Say: " Wait a moment. I want to surprise you. Look at the goods first, so that you will see what you're getting for the money." Then, when you have given him a high opinion of the goods, tell him the price.

The customer, naturally, thinks mainly of price. You must not accept his point of view. You must think mainly of the value of the goods.

If you are selling watches, for instance, you will first hand a watch to the customer. Then you will point out its good qualities until the customer thinks it is $10. Then you tell him the price is $7. And you are sure to make a sale.

But if, on the contrary, he glances at the watch and thinks it is worth $5, and if you tell him at once that the price is $7, he will not give you an order. " It is too dear," he thinks. He sees himself losing $2 per watch.

In every sale a great deal of the technique consists in doing first things first; and telling the price comes at the end of the selling process, never at the beginning.

If you must mention a figure at the beginning of the conversation, mention a higher figure. Say: " Now, here is a regular $2 line, as you can see. Notice the workmanship. Hold it up to the light. And I can let you have it for $1.50. It ought to sell easily at $2.75."

You are talking to him in terms of quality and profit. You are showing him what he will make, not what he will have to pay you. That is the correct way.

Price, you see, is mental. It is dear if the customer thinks it is; and it is cheap if the customer thinks it is.

A customer who will object to paying an extra nickel for a bottle of ink will gladly pay $25 for a seat at a prize-fight.

A wealthy woman who will object to paying what she thinks is a 10-cent overcharge on a laundry bill will joyfully pay $150 for an antique chair.

A man will go and buy an automobile for the price of a 7-room house, and he will not for a moment think that the car is dear. He is so keen to have it that he writes out the check cheerfully.

It is a curious fact that people will pay a high price for luxuries, while they hold tight to every cent when they are buying necessities.

They make far more fuss about the price of a cabbage than they do about the price of a bottle of wine. They will pay $5 for a theater ticket much more readily than they will pay 60 cents for a pound of sausages.

It is not the amount of the price that matters. It is the way the customer feels about it.

Consequently, before mentioning price, you must get him into a mood of desire. You must prepare his mind before you give him the price. All this seems simple enough, but it is not done in 90 per cent. of the selling, either by travelers or store clerks.

The reason that it is not done, is because

the salesman does not know much about his goods, and, to tell the truth, is somewhat bored and fed up with them.

The traveler must know his goods through and through — how they are made, the wonderful machines that made them, how they compare with competitive goods, how they wear and the distinguished people who are now using them.

He must have a certain amount of enthusiasm for his goods — the more the better.

A true salesman, in fact, compels the customer to appreciate the goods. He gives the point of view of the goods. He points out the pleasures of ownership. He is the Spokesman of the goods.

When he is selling a fur coat, for instance, he says what the coat would say for itself if it had a voice. He points out that a fur coat is the queen of women's garments. He shows that it is more than fur — more than a coat. It gives a higher social status to the fortunate woman who wears it.

That is why a salesman must have a trained

imagination. He must see what the customer does not see, and he must be able to make the customer see what he sees. He must be able to wake up the customer out of his daze, and compel him to appreciate the merits and the marvels of the goods.

A salesman must not only Talk about quality. He must dramatize it. He must prove it. He must show by test and demonstration the superior quality of his goods.

Very often, the goods are better than they look. A first glance at them does not tell you how valuable they are.

Once, for instance, I was called in to plan a campaign to sell etchings by a famous French artist. These etchings were very valuable, but the artist's name was unknown in Britain and America.

At first glance, these etchings looked outrageously dear and the salesmen reported that the price was far too high.

So, to demonstrate their value, I had a special picture frame made for every salesman. At the top of each frame were three high-power electric lights under a hood. And the etchings could be readily put in these frames, or taken out.

The salesmen were offering the etchings direct to business men, for their homes. They were not trying to sell to dealers.

Armed with a hooded frame, a salesman would go into a business man's office, pull down the curtains, connect the frame with an electric light, and, in a darkened room, a blaze of light would fall directly upon the etching.

This is what we call dramatizing a sale. It creates curiosity, appreciation, desire. It is not a trick. It is a legitimate device to display goods of high quality. In this case, we sold all our etchings, at a slightly higher price.

A customer, may I say, is one who wants the goods more often than he wants the price. There is the central fact around which all Salesmanship is built.

How to increase the " want " of the customer, in some other way than by lowering the price — that is the problem.

To make a sale by cutting the price — to

make a sale by giving away the profit — is not salesmanship at all. If persevered in, it is bankruptcy.

Salesmanship means selling goods at a fair profit to customers who are satisfied.

There is a pair of scales, as we might say, in the customer's mind. On the one side of the scales there is the price and on the other side is the article to be sold.

What, then, can be done to tip the scales in favor of the article? That is the vital point.

Every well-made article has a definite number of quality-points of design, style, durability, limited quantity, new features, etc. The salesman must have these at the tip of his tongue.

Quality, in a word, is like a ladder. It has different rungs, or grades, like this:

Artistic.
Original.
Superior.
Good.
Good Enough.
Half Good.
No Good.

The great bulk of cheap goods are " good enough." They have a few quality-points, not many.

But " good " merchandise has points of quality that must be pointed out, if it is to be sold.

The tragedy of merchandising is to be compelled to sell " good " merchandise at " good enough " prices. That happens for lack of salesmanship.

The price goes up by leaps and bounds when you move towards the top of the ladder. An " artistic " gown is worth ten times the price of a " good " gown, for instance. The Paris dressmakers know that.

Just as a chess player works out new moves to beat his opponent — just as a jockey works out a better way to handle a difficult horse — so a salesman must work out new ways of showing the quality of his goods, so that, when he tells the price, the customer will prefer the goods to the money.

V

DON'T TAKE " NO " FOR A FINAL ANSWER

CHAPTER V

DON'T TAKE " NO " FOR A FINAL ANSWER

Difference Between Making and Taking a Sale — Some Examples of Real Salesmanship

CAN I sell you anything to-day? " said a traveling salesman to a shopkeeper.

" No," replied the shopkeeper.

" All right," replied the traveler, " I'll call next month.   Good morning! "   And out he went.

That sort of thing is supposed to be called SALESMANSHIP.

That traveler may even have had a belief that it was his DUTY to leave as soon as the shopkeeper said " No."

He took " No " as his cue to go out, whereas, if he had been a trained salesman, he would have taken " No " as his cue to BEGIN SELL-ING.

The fact is, that real professional salesmanship starts when the customer says " No."

If a customer says " Yes," then no salesmanship is needed. Any order-taker will do.

THE WHOLE OBJECT OF SALESMANSHIP IS TO CHANGE NEGATIVES INTO AFFIRMATIVES.

If a salesman cannot face a " No " and change it into a " Yes," then he is a round peg in a square hole.

Salesmanship is persuasion. It is the overcoming of difficulties. It is an advance in the face of an attack.

There is an element of WAR in salesmanship, but with this great difference — the customer must not be forced to do what he will regret.

A professional salesman conquers a customer by taking the customer's point of view. He shows the shopkeeper how to sell. He cheers up the shopkeeper and gives him a plan for selling more goods.

A real salesman is the shopkeeper's best friend. He comes to the shopkeeper as a man comes to a run-down clock. He cleans the dis-

couragement out of his mind, winds him up
and starts him going.

THE MAN WE NEED AT THE MOMENT, MORE
THAN ANYONE ELSE, IS THE SALESMAN WHO
CAN CHANGE " NO " INTO " YES " AND START
THE WHEELS OF TRADE SPINNING AT FULL
SPEED.

" The best sale I ever made," said W. S.
English, a well-known traveler, " was on one
occasion when I turned a man's ' No ' into
' Yes.'

" I was selling gas mantles. My firm made
a good mantle, but did not advertise very
much. Their mantles had more quality than
fame.

" My firm was very anxious to sell to a certain Mr. Long. He had steadfastly refused to
buy from us, as he was a regular customer of a
rival firm.

" I went to Mr. Long, gave him the usual
sales talk. No result. He said: ' I'll make up
my mind this evening. Call on me to-morrow
morning at 9 o'clock and I will give you my
decision.'

" Of course, I knew what that meant. It meant ' No.' He was trying to let me down easy.

" I made up my mind that I must do something different. I felt sure that Mr. Long was not convinced of the quality of our mantles.

" I had only TALKED about quality, but I hadn't proved it. This seemed to me to be the weakness of my salesmanship.

" I pondered over the matter for two hours. Then I had an idea. It flashed on my mind like a gleam of light.

" I rushed out of the hotel and bought a pair of apothecary scales, and an assortment of mantles of various makes.

" Then, next morning at 9 o'clock, I went to see Mr. Long. As I had expected, he said ' No.'

" I didn't fade away as most salesmen do when they get struck by a ' No.' I said: ' Very well, Mr. Long, but if I can prove to you that price for price my mantles are the best, will you reconsider your decision? '

" He was kind enough to agree, so we went into his office. I took out my scales and all the mantles.

" One by one I weighed the mantles. Then I burned them and re-weighed them.

" I was taking a chance on what the result would be, but I had faith in my firm. I knew that our factory put quality first.

" When we compared figures, I had proved my case. Our mantles had more actual thorium and cerium oxide than those of our competitors. Price for price, ours were plainly the best.

" Mr. Long was convinced. He said ' Yes,' and I went off at 10 o'clock with an order for 10,000 mantles."

There is a vast difference, as you can see, between MAKING a sale and merely TAKING it.

When a customer wants to buy before you come to him, that is only TAKING a sale; but when he didn't think of buying until you showed him that he ought to, that is MAKING a sale.

On one occasion a young salesman, who sells

furniture for a wholesale house, went into a mining town.

He found that the largest shop in town was packed full of goods, and, also, he found that the shopkeeper was packed full of the blues.

" Well," said the salesman, " I see I can't sell you anything, but perhaps I can help you to get rid of all this stuff.

" Let's take half-a-dozen phonographs in a motor truck and sell them to the miners."

They motored to a mining village fifteen miles away and sold five phonographs. The next day they sold twelve in other villages.

The salesman went away with a $1,500 order. That was a case of MAKING a sale.

Here is another case. A biscuit salesman had tried for two years to sell his goods to the chief grocer in a New England town, but without success.

At last, the light broke in on his mind. He saw that he must MAKE a sale, not take it.

He went into this grocer's shop and asked — " Will you sell a carload of biscuits for us, Mr. Gray? "

Mr. Gray was swept off his feet. Of course, he would sell a carload of biscuits, but how?

The salesman had a Plan — a one week BISCUIT SALE, prepared for by a week of free samples.

The grocer wrote an order for half a carload, sold it all and ordered more. That sale was MADE, not taken.

The fact is, that nine salesmen out of ten approach a dealer in the wrong way. They talk BUYING not SELLING. There is a world of difference, if you'll give it a moment of thought. When a dealer BUYS, he pays out money. But when he SELLS, he takes in money.

That is why no dealer likes to talk about buying, and why every dealer loves to talk about selling.

If you want to learn the profitable art of MAKING sales, you must study your customer's point of view.

Making a sale doesn't mean compelling a customer to take what he doesn't want. It means getting him to appreciate the goods and to see what he can do with them.

A salesman who was selling plots of lana was given 48 plots to sell near a beach. The land was eight minutes' walk from the station.

The salesman walked his prospects to the plots and then took them down to the beach, a quarter of a mile distant.

Nobody bought. Most of them did not go to the beach. So the salesman changed his methods.

He took each prospect in a taxi to the beach first. He sold them on the beach. Then he showed the plots and walked back to the station.

In a short time he sold all the 48 plots. Those 48 sales were made, not taken.

So, the fact that I wish to make clear is that the SALESMAN MUST BE ACTIVE, CREATIVE, SUGGESTIVE, POSITIVE.

Standing still, looking bored and answering questions as briefly as possible, isn't Salesmanship — not on your life it isn't.

Turning yourself into an imitation of a penny-in-the-slot machine, isn't Salesmanship.

Standing behind a glove counter and wishing

you could go far away and never see a pair of gloves again as long as you lived, isn't Salesmanship.

Traveling from door to door with a detested bag of samples and fading out as soon as a dealers says " No," isn't Salesmanship.

No, but thousands of sales people think it is. They expect to be paid for this sort of thing.

They would be very much offended if they were paid in Tin money at the end of the week; but they give this sort of Tin Salesmanship to their firms.

They can only TAKE a sale when a customer gives it to them. They cannot MAKE a sale.

They are negative, passive, mechanical and indifferent.

Give us sales people who can make sales and half of our business troubles will disappear.

To sum up, there is always more or less BUYER-RESISTANCE. In good times there is less of it and in bad times there is more. But there is always resistance, and much of it can be overcome.

Thousands of customers say " No " as a

habit. Every experienced salesman knows that. It is a habit of self-protection, or pocket-protection. They say " No " to give themselves time to think.

Therefore, when a man says " No," his refusal should not be taken as final. The conversation may be switched to another subject, but the attempt at selling should not be abandoned.

A salesman should have the perseverance of a scientist. He should be deaf to that disastrous word " No."

He should be like those boxers who fight all the better after they have been knocked down.

He should never forget that a strong man makes a ladder out of his failures, not a wall. He climbs up over obstacles. He does not turn back. He keeps on until the resistance is overcome, or until he finds out that there are good reasons for the resistance.

VI

GET DOWN TO BRASS TACKS
QUICKLY

CHAPTER VI

GET DOWN TO BRASS TACKS QUICKLY

Watch for Chance to Talk — Details of Delivery — Technique of Making a Sale.

TOO many traveling salesmen are like the parrot that " talked too —— much." They keep on talking when the chance has come to be writing down orders.

Many a salesman talks a customer into a sale and then goes on and talks him out of it.

The right technique in making a sale is this: First listen to the customer, then talk to him about his affairs, from his point of view, then get him interested in your goods.

As soon as he shows desire for your goods, it is wisest to take it for granted that he has made up his mind to buy.

You should then stop pointing out quality.

You should as quickly as lightning change the conversation to details of delivery.

You should ask about assortment or quantity or time of shipment or any other detail, in order to get the customer's mind definitely made up.

To use a simile from the carpenter's trade, you should clinch the nail the moment it comes through the board.

You should say, " I can let you have 10 gross of these." Certainly you must not say, " How many do you want? "

Too often a salesman forces a customer into a corner and compels him to say " Yes " or " No." This shows a lack of skill. It usually makes the customer say " No."

A salesman should take it for granted that the customer wants the goods, just as soon as this seems to be true.

He then says, at once: " Would you prefer to have them sent by motor, instead of by rail? "

" Do you want them for next Monday's Sale? "

" Shall I send our new Window Display with it? " or any similar question.

A salesman must, in this way, do all that he can to prevent a customer from feeling that he has surrendered.

He must talk as though this were a matter of mutual interest, as indeed it is. He must not assume an attitude of forcing the customer to buy.

One salesman, for instance, who came into my office to sell me a new kind of a typewriter, first secured my interest by a very clever demonstration, and then spoiled it all by saying, " Well, I can't sell you one, can I? " Of course I said " No." If he had said " I can leave this one with you, if you'd like to have it at once," I would probably have bought it.

The fact is that many salesman are good at opening a sale but bad at closing. There are some salesmen so clever that they can get in to see anybody, but after they have got in they do not make a sale. Every big concern has lost money on salesmen of this sort.

They are always men of pleasing appearance, good education and great fluency. They are sociable, too, and quick to make friends.

By means of all these good qualities, they secure an interview. They get favorable attention — and that is all they get.

They have a pleasant conversation which ends in nothing but a " Good-bye! Call again." They go away without an order.

They make hundreds of " almost " sales. They often impress their employers, for a time, as being first-class salesmen. But their order books tell the tale.

They are about 80 per cent. salesmen. If they could only learn to close, to bring matters to a head, they would rise to par.

Favorable attention, you see, is not enough. A salesman must be an entertainer, up to a point. He must appear to be making a social call, if you like, until the psychological moment comes to get the order. Then he must suddenly turn into a man of facts and figures and details.

He must be able to get down to brass tacks in a flash.

Having a good time with a customer is all very well as far as it goes, but it doesn't go far enough.

If a customer says, " I will let you know next week," or " I'll think it over," that sale is lost, 99 times out of 100. Every experienced salesman knows that.

Promises yield no dividends. They pay no salaries and no profits. Nothing has been done until the order is in the book.

Always, a salesman must do all he can to prevent this postponement of a decision. He must not accept it as the end of the interview.

One very able salesman, for instance, called on a business man and convinced him that he needed a better office equipment. The business man plainly wanted the new equipment, but he was by nature a postponer. He said to the salesman: " This is a large matter. It involves too much money to close at once."

The salesman replied, " Mr. Smith, is it not true that a deal of this size is a mere trifle for your company? Do you really need to postpone it? Can you not decide it right away just as you do other important matters? ''

He got the order — he deserved it.

Many a customer has an inbred dislike to saying " Yes." He prefers always to appoint a committee, or to put some of the responsibility on some one else.

He has more authority than experience, probably, as many executives have. This makes him non-committal. He is always aiming at safety rather than net profit.

Many men have vague, hazy brains — twilight brains. Their wills are weak and swayed more by fears than hopes.

As you can see, to sell goods to such brains requires great decisiveness on the part of the salesman. If he, too, is a drifter and a postponer, nothing will be done.

Few customers know their own minds. They act only when pushed. They follow the line of most compulsion and least resistance all through life.

For this reason, a salesman must take control of the interview. He must not play second fiddle, although he may seem to be doing so.

A salesman is not a mere conversationalist. He knows when to converse and when to shut up. He uses conversation as a tool.

What he is concerned with is the process that is going on in the mind of the customer. And he is determined that this process shall end in an order.

He is an order-getter, not a propagandist nor a collector of kind words.

In every sale the fewer words the better. Suppose, for instance, that a man is selling his services as an efficiency expert. Suppose that he is called in by a board of directors, whose main idea is to pump him dry and let him go, what should he do?

Certainly, he should not make a sales talk. The odds are against him. They can easily out-talk him. They can make game of him with foolish questions.

He should take it for granted that they want his services. He should say, pleasantly, " Yes,

I shall be glad to do this work for you.   I can give you Wednesdays."

He should press them for details as to what, where and when.   Then, before any talk can begin, he should pick up his hat and leave.

Almost always, too much time and talk are spent in making a sale.   And too many sales are talked off as well as on.

A keen salesman will be on the watch for his chance to ask for the details of delivery.

He will close off the sales interview by a busy five minutes of order-taking.   As soon as he has a nibble, he will jerk.   That is what I mean.

This one Tip, studied and carried out by any competent salesman, will make two orders grow where only one grew before.

VII

BUILD GOODWILL FOR YOUR FIRM

CHAPTER VII

BUILD GOODWILL FOR YOUR FIRM

*Sell Your Company as Well as Your Goods —
How to Earn Promotion*

IT goes without saying that a salesman should never let his company down. When he stands in front of a customer, his creed must be: " My company, right or wrong."

If there are any confessions or excuses to be made, let them come from the Sales Manager — from the home office.

A salesman must admit freely what he cannot honestly deny, but he must always defend his firm, just as a lawyer must always defend his client before the judge.

Stand like a rock, if you are met with a flood of complaints.

Don't assume that the customer is right. Assume nothing. Say: " I will have all this investigated; and you may rely upon my company to put matters right."

Never agree with a customer when he blames your house. Many salesmen do, with the intention of pleasing the customer.

Often a salesman will say, in disgust, " There! That is the third time in this week that the clerks in our office have made a blunder — the wooden-heads."

That is what he FEELS like saying. That is probably the truth. But it is not a wise thing to say.

A salesman should try to speak from the point of view of the customer. He should " talk him." But not against his own concern.

The man who lowers his concern lowers himself still more.

For his own sake, a traveling salesman must fight his company's battles and guard its interests.

Even though his customer may feel annoyed at him, at the moment, the customer will respect him all the more for taking the company's part.

A salesman who accepts blame, as though he were the head of the house, is a much larger man to the eyes of the customer than a salesman who joins in the attack on his own company.

Whether you remain with the company or not, no matter. Stand by it as long as its money is in your pocket.

All the world despises a Judas who betrays his Master for 30 pieces of silver; and a man is certainly as bad as Judas when he betrays the concern that has honored him with its confidence and its money.

Loyalty is always and everywhere a virtue that everyone respects. It is a virtue among savage and civilized nations. It has always been a virtue and it always will be. It has not been abolished nor modified by this Age of Trade and Commerce.

" Every man for himself " — yes, up to a point. The question is: Does any man help his own interests by letting his concern down? He does not.

If a salesman finds that his company is dishonest or unreliable, then his one best policy is to resign and find another employer that can be depended upon. No salesman can do good work if he is ashamed of his employer.

A salesman owes it to himself to work for a concern that he can trust and respect.

The best concerns make blunders at times. They send the wrong goods or the wrong bill or something of the sort.

They make clerical errors, or errors that arise from the carelessness of a new employee; and when these mistakes are made, the salesman must stand by his house and insist that all errors will be corrected.

A salesman is never guilty of bad taste when he praises his employer. He is like a football player, who can praise his team without being accused of egotism.

Usually, in sports, it is team-play that makes a team win; and the same fact is true of a business organization.

The spirit of team-play — the company feeling — goes far to make an organization successful.

The salesman who runs away to a competing firm and takes his customers with him, or tries to do so, is not respected, even by the concern that takes him on.

There are rules of fair play and decent conduct in business, just as there are in sport. And, in the long run, the man who breaks these rules suffers for it.

Goodwill! That is the main thing. It is more than money, because it is the basis of credit.

The salesman who builds up his firm's goodwill will soon create a goodwill of his own. That is the vital point to remember.

Every day of his life, a salesman is either increasing or decreasing the goodwill of his company.

By his appearance, his methods, his talk, a salesman is adding to or subtracting from his company's assets. That may not be a comfortable thought. But it is a fact that ought to be remembered.

The traveling salesman who says, proudly, " I have the best employer in the world," does not do himself any damage and he is not set down as a braggart.

To say this is not always easy, especially after he has had a long, fault-finding letter from his Sales Manager, as often happens. But the traveler who can keep his loyalty red-hot, in spite of splashes of cold water, will do well for his employer and himself, both.

Goodwill must come first. It must even come before sales, if there should be any clash between the two.

A sale should never be made at the expense of goodwill — that is a fact that many a concern forgets, when it has dead stock to get rid of.

A traveling salesman, in fact, is much more than a salesman. He really is an agent — an intermediary — a commercial ambassador. There is no word in the English language to properly define him.

He is not merely selling goods. He is building up the reputation of his organization. He is not at all like a door-to-door canvasser, who represents nobody, and whose one aim is to make a sale.

A traveler represents his company. He is the whole company, legally, as he stands in front of a customer. The company is responsible for what he says and does.

The company is the body and he is one of the finger-ends. He is a vital part of his firm. He is not a hireling. He is not a messenger — a carrier of samples.

" I am Brown and Smith, Incorporated," he can truly say.

No other member of the organization is in the same favored position as a traveling salesman. He is not supervised, as a foreman or a shop assistant is.

He is on his own. He does not work in his company's building. He is trusted to regulate his own hours.

He is a free and independent man of business, as long as he does well. He is judged by results.

If he is paid on commission, as he should be, he is practically on the same footing as an owner, although he has not invested any capital in the company. He gets his full fair share of the profits. He is not at all a wage-worker. He takes his own risks, plans and performs his own work and gets all that he earns.

Consequently, as he is practically a partner, he should take a partner's interest in the prosperity of his concern.

He may not always be a salesman. He may become Sales Manager — President. Many a man has climbed up from the position of traveling salesman to the presidency of his firm.

Promotion! That is to be considered, as well as salary and commission. And the way to become a high executive is to act like one and keep it up.

So, it is always a wise policy, after the last order has been taken, to say a few words about your people. Surely there is one sentence that can be said in praise of one's own organization.

" By the way, you may be pleased to know that our new factory is finished," some such news as this will always come to mind.

A man cannot blow his own horn without

being a bit of a bore; but he can blow his company's horn. He can talk for two minutes as though he were its president.

Also, a salesman can serve his company by sending back to the Sales Manager the opinions of customers, or any item of news regarding them.

If a shop is falling into decay, he can mention the fact in one of his letters.

He can take note of any new progressive store and notice whether it is likely to prosper or to be a mushroom growth.

If salesmen did their full duty, there would be fewer of these frauds whereby goods are bought, sold at a low price and never paid for.

A salesman can do much, too, to create public opinion about his organization.

There may be a misunderstanding about it. It may have a bad name, undeservedly, for something it is believed to have done in the past.

During the war, for instance, many concerns were compelled to lower the quality of their goods. They were obliged to use substitutes. Their goodwill was seriously injured. Any such matter as this can be dealt with by traveling salesmen, as they go up and down among the customers.

So, it is clear that a salesman has a wide scope for his efforts, when he tries to sell his organization as well as the goods.

VIII

CONSTANTLY SEARCH FOR NEW MARKETS

Chapter VIII

CONSTANTLY SEARCH FOR NEW MARKETS

Make Several Missionary Calls Every Week — Don't Become a Jog-Trotter

IT is a strange fact that among traveling salesmen the oldest will bring in the fewest new accounts. When a traveler has been nine or ten years with a company he has become well acquainted with its customers. He is made welcome. He is given cigars. The customers listen to his stories; and his business has become largely a matter of visiting his friends.

Consequently, he does not like to dig up new customers. He has become dignified. He is proud of his position as one of the Senior Salesmen of his house. He does not like to have anyone ask him what his name is; and thus he brings in very few new accounts.

A young chap, on the contrary, who has no friends and no dignity and no past career with the company, will usually bring in more new accounts than anybody else.

Once, a firm of jewelers had a contest among its salesmen, to see who could bring in the greatest number of new accounts.

There was a keen young man at the telephone switchboard. He was not a salesman. He had never sold anything in his life.

He asked permission to enter the contest. To please him, the concern agreed. Then, to the amazement of everyone, he won the prize against 30 experienced traveling salesmen.

Naturally, not having any regular customers, this young man went into every jewelery shop. He probably had more refusals than any of the other salesmen, but he opened up the greatest number of new accounts.

You will find it to be a general rule, that the older a salesman is in point of service, the fewer new accounts he will open up.

The old, experienced traveler will generally

bring in the largest orders, but not very many new customers.

He will justify himself by all manner of very clever excuses, but when his place is taken by a younger man, new customers are invariably found. Often, the volume of business is doubled.

He goes into a town and gets $1,000 worth of orders, whereas he might have got $2,000 worth if he had searched for new customers.

Over and over again, concerns have found that plenty of absolutely new business can be dug up in a territory which is supposed to be well canvassed.

Every traveling salesman goes past too many doors. When he arrives in a town, he at once thinks of a certain number of houses. HE MAKES HIS USUAL ROUND — that is the danger that confronts every salesman.

Unless he is on his guard, every traveling salesman becomes more or less an automaton. He gets into a rut. Why? Because a rut is always easier and requires no thought.

Most men prefer the smooth broad path,

that leads nowhere in particular, instead of the rough narrow path that leads upwards to success.

It is a fact, known to everyone, that there are too many jog-trot travelers, jogging from town to town and getting only the easy orders.

They send in just enough orders to keep themselves from being sacked, but nobody makes any profit on them except the railways and hotels.

They take the orders that regular customers give them, and they imagine that they are doing their full duty as salesman.

They never make a fight to get new business. They never invent new ways to makes sales.

Recently I heard a remarkable story about an insurance company that changed its traveling salesmen from jog-trotters to record-breakers. It can be done.

To begin with, this company had 1,700 travelers or salesmen in 1913, who produced $20,000,000 of business.

To-day, it has 375 salesmen, who produced last year $52,000,000.

In 1913, its average salesman produced $11,750 in orders a year.

To-day its average salesman produces $137,-325.

The selling power of each salesman was multiplied by eleven.

How was it done?

First, it tested all its traveling salesmen — tested them by studying their records and by personal examination.

It found that its best salesmen were the married ones, 33 to 38 years old, who belonged to a number of organizations and had saved money.

It found that college education was not important, and that the main thing was the ambition and energy and sense of the man himself.

Second, it trained the men that it picked out. It spent, all told, $1,000 on every man to make him highly skilled in the art of salesmanship.

It weeded out the jog-trotters, and to-day its business is 250 per cent. higher than it used to be.

Tests like this prove that every body of

traveling salesmen needs to be kept alive and alert. It must not be allowed to drift along, neither for its own sake nor the company's sake.

There must be a constant search for new markets. If your present distributors are not doing their share, then new distributors must be found.

Stagnation must never be accepted as a normal condition — how few companies realize that!

Every company loses customers. Consequently, every company must secure new customers to make up for their losses. The company that loses fifty customers a year and gains forty is on its way to the graveyard.

There is a word called " saturation," which is doing many concerns a great deal of harm. " We have reached the point of saturation in selling our goods to Detroit," says a Sales Manager.

How does he know? Has he any data or does he merely say this because it pleases the executives?

The point of saturation is not a FIXED point. It depends upon salesmanship. The demand can be doubled — perhaps trebled, by skillful selling and advertising.

You will often hear a salesman say: " No, I never go there. They do not buy from us." He makes this absurd remark as though it were wise — as though it were a legitimate excuse.

Once, when I was traveling, I was having a chat with a traveling salesman. He got off at Chicago.

" Well, good-bye," he said, " I have to see three concerns here."

Why three? The same old three concerns, no doubt, that he had been calling on for five years!

Surely, in a busy city like Chicago there ought to be more than three customers for his goods. Surely he had not saturated Chicago when he made three sales.

On another occasion I asked a manufacturer how many customers he had.

" About 7,000," he replied.

" And how many haven't you got? " I

asked. He was surprised. He didn't know. An investigation was made and it was found that there were 18,000 customers he HADN'T got. Yet he had reached the point of saturation, in his opinion.

So, is it not clear that a traveling salesman must do a certain amount of creative work every week? Is it not clear that he should never let a week go by without an attempt to put new names on his list?

If he is selling to retail shops, he can try several new streets every week. If he is selling to manufacturers, he can follow the line of chimneys, instead of the line of old customers.

It is a wise plan to try experiments on non-customers instead of on regular buyers. There is less to lose if the experiment fails.

In a word, every keen, ambitious traveler must do missionary work for at least half-a-day a week.

He must not allow himself to become like a postman, jogging along from one familiar door to another, as though there were not scores of possible customers whom he is passing by.

For his own sake and his employer's sake, he should develop the possibilities of his territory, and not settle down to the unprofitable opinion that the sales he is making are all that can be made.

Now and then, he might spend a whole week in calling on non-customers and none else. That would be a week well spent.

IX

CLASSIFY YOUR TIME

CHAPTER IX

CLASSIFY YOUR TIME

*How to Value the Different Hours of the Day
— The Best Time to Make a Sale*

A CERTAIN employer called his forty traveling salesmen together recently and made the following speech:

" Gentlemen, I have been making some interesting calculations, which are just as important to you as to me.

" They explain, in fact, why I cannot raise your salaries and why I cannot afford a Roll-Royce this year.

" I find that the actual number of days you worked last year was 265. You average 100 days off for Sundays, holidays and illness.

" Allowing 8 hours a day, this means 2,120 hours. But this is not your actual selling time.

" I find that you have averaged 6 calls a day — 32 calls a week. These calls average 15 minutes each.

" But only half of the calls result in real interviews, so that leaves only 16 interviews a week.

" Only half of these interviews resulted in sales. That means that your actual selling time last year was 8 times 15 minutes or, Two Hours a Week.

" You are costing me in salaries alone about $50 per hour, apiece, for actual selling time. This seems incredible, but I cannot find any error in these figures. Can any one of you show me where I am wrong? "

The salesmen were silent. There was nothing to be said. It was true.

But the next week their Sales went up 30 per cent.

This was an extreme case. But the fact is that the average actual selling time of traveling salesmen is not far from two hours a day.

In a 300-day year, for instance, a traveler usually spends about 75 days in actual selling.

He spends 110 days traveling. He is well named a traveler, for he travels more than he sells. He is the railway's best friend. Also, he spends 50 days writing, in offices and lobbies; and 65 days doing clerical work.

" Talk about an 8-hour day," says a Sales Manager. " If I could get my travelers to do a 4-hour day, they would sell twice as much goods as they do now."

And this is not the worst of it.

Not only does a traveler lose 6 hours out of the 8-hour day. Often, he does worse. He loses the BEST 3 hours. He loses the precious time between 12 and 1 and between 2 and 4.

These three hours, in my opinion, are worth almost double as much as the other 5 hours of day.

The PEAK of the day, in value — in possibilities of selling — is the hour between 2 and 3.

THIS IS THE GOLDEN HOUR FOR ALL TRAVELING SALESMEN.

If I were putting a value on the various hours of the day, I would price them as follows:

9 to 10	....	5
10 to 11	....	10
11 to 12	....	20
12 to 1	....	40
1 to 2	....	10
2 to 3	....	60
3 to 4	....	40
4 to 5	....	20
5 to 6	....	10
6 to 7	....	5

A day ought to be cut up, in fact, in the same way that a butcher cuts up a bullock. Some parts of the bullock will be sold for 40 cents a pound and other parts will be sold for 20 cents a pound.

The hour between 2 and 3 is the one best hour to sell goods for the reason that the customer is feeling more amiable and sociable at that time than at any other hour of the day.

Some men are so irascible that they should never be seen except after lunch. Every experienced salesman knows that. This hour seems to be the only time when some men are human.

After lunch, a business man has got rid of the most pressing worries of the day. He has escaped from his infernal correspondence, with its demands and complaints.

Also, he has had his lunch, and that means that his brain has slowed down. His subconscious brain is giving its attention to his stomach, not to his cerebrum. He is digesting rather than thinking. His mind and his will are relaxed. He is less aggressive and more friendly.

He is easier to approach and to convince. He will listen to you. He will give you his WHOLE mind, not 10 per cent. of it, as he is apt to do if you bother him between 9 and 10.

On the whole, he is rather pleased to see you between 2 and 3, as he is in the humor for a talk with some one.

So the problem, so far as time is concerned, is how to spend the most favorable hours in actual selling.

If a traveler sees no one between 9 and 10, no matter. If he sees no one between 10 and 11 or between 5 and 6, there is little lost. But if he wastes the Golden Hour, from 2 to 3, then more than a quarter of his day has gone.

The secret of an efficient day, to a traveling salesman, is to be actually selling goods from 11 to 1 and from 2 to 4. These 4 precious hours must not be used for traveling, waiting or clerical work.

This new formula, which I am here presenting to traveling salesmen, might be worded as follows:

Classify your time according to its value, and spend the most valuable hours in meeting customers, and not in traveling, waiting and clerical work.

From 2 to 3 is the tidbit of the day. Save it from wastage.

I have heard old buffalo hunters say that they often would kill a buffalo merely for his tongue. They left all the rest of the buffalo to the coyotes. They took only the tidbit, when meat was plentiful.

In the same way, travelers should regard that hour — 2 to 3 — as the most precious bit of the day. They should not waste it, as I have often seen them do, in drowsy siestas in the hotels.

Is it true that the Big Event of the day to many salesmen is the hour from 2 to 3? No. It is the hour and a half from 1 to 2:30. The Big Event is LUNCH.

Lunch is the Peak. It is the comfort — the consolation. Many a salesman anticipates it for 2 hours and regrets it for another 2 hours.

He eats a thick slice of roast beef, two big potatoes, a plate of cabbage and a slice of pie, after which he becomes torpid for an hour. That's what happens to at least the first half of the Golden Hour.

An efficient salesman, on the contrary, eats a light lunch. At 6:30 or 7 P.M., after his day's work is done, he can have his big dinner — as big as he wishes.

A traveler, in a word, must keep himself fit. He is not a routine worker. He is not an automaton. A day's work, to a traveler, is like running a race, or playing a game. It is a contest — brain against brain. That is why he should not gorge himself just before the most important hour of the day arrives.

Whenever possible, he should take a customer to lunch. That will be making a good use of the 1 to 2 hour.

In some trades, the best hour may be 4 to 5, or 10 to 11, but the general principle still holds true. The hours of the day are not alike in value to any salesman.

The use of his time is left to him. He is not like a school teacher, following a schedule, or like a railway engine driver, keeping to a time-table that has been arranged for him.

He should plan his day. Every evening he should plan to-morrow. He should never let a day crash on him unawares.

Many traveling salesmen have grown into the habit of writing off Monday morning and Saturday morning. Nothing can be done, they say, on these two unfortunate mornings.

Neither can they make sales, they believe, before 11 A.M., nor after 5 P.M., nor between 1 and 2; nor when the customer is busy, nor when he is out of temper. These travelers gradually come to an end, because they avoid all the difficulties.

If it is true that certain mornings and hours are of no value as selling hours, then a traveler should manage to do some other work in these hours and concentrate his full selling force into the good hours.

There is no reason why a salesman should waste his traveling time and his waiting time, as many do.

Plans can be made on the train, and in a waiting room. A traveler can always have a book in his pocket — a novel or a text-book.

Many salesmen object to being managed in detail by the home office. Some of them rejoice in their freedom, but they do not make a good use of their freedom.

They are like the young salesman who, when he was first sent out on the road, wrote back home to his mother and said:

" I am my own master and I am taking orders from no one." Very likely.

If a traveler can be set free to manage himself, he will be all the better for it, if he is the right sort. I do not believe in handling travelers as though they were busses — as though they wore pedometers and were paid on mileage. If they are driven to make a fixed number of calls per day, they are apt to be made into nervous wrecks or liars, more likely the latter.

Manage yourself. Then you will not be harried by the home office.

Divide up your day. Use the best hours for selling. Don't waste the tidbits of your time.

Efficiency means getting a higher percentage of result — a better result with less energy.

As you can see, the best way for a traveler to increase his efficiency is to classify his time, so that he doesn't waste his best hours on his smallest jobs, or endanger his best sales by trying to make them at the wrong time.

How to fit the hour to the job, so as to make the best possible use of a day — it is not easy. No. But it is profitable and it can be done.

X

KEEP MENTALLY AND PHYSICALLY FIT

CHAPTER X

KEEP MENTALLY AND PHYSICALLY FIT

Vaccinate Yourself Against Worries — Your Job Is Not a Routine One — It Is All Creative Work

IT is the brain behind the samples that makes the sales. A traveling saleman is not a legger. He is not a coolie, though he often feels as though he were, as he lugs his heavy suitcases about.

He is a brain-worker, much more so than an architect is, as a salesman's brain is in a constant struggle with other brains.

A salesman does not deal with facts, designs, ideas, employees. No. Nothing so easy as that. He deals with other people, over whom he has no control.

His work is very exhausting. He uses up

more energy than most brain workers do. He needs an hour more sleep every night than an ordinary man does.

Isn't it true that many a salesman is all fagged out by Friday afternoon? Isn't it true that he hasn't a kick left in him by Saturday morning. Ask any salesman's wife. She knows.

He eats all sorts of meals. He sleeps in all sorts of beds. He has to deal with all sorts of people. He is all day long in the midst of strangers, fighting a lone battle on behalf of himself and his firm. As you can see, it is very necessary for him to keep fit.

A salesman who stumbles into a busy merchant's office, with a tired body and a jaded brain and fishy eyes, isn't very likely to get an order, is he?

He may try to excuse himself. He may say, " Sorry, Mr. Jones, but I'm a little off color this morning." But what does Jones care? No business man likes to have his office invaded by nervous wrecks.

No. You cannot cut with dull tools. You

must be sharp and well tempered if you want to make money selling goods on commission.

You cannot handle difficult customers if you have a quart of food in your stomach.

You cannot handle him if your brain is crying out for four hours more sleep.

If you sat up until 2 A. M. playing cards, you are about as much use at 10 A. M. as a drunkard.

Thirty or forty years ago, it was customary, in some trades, for the customer and the salesman first to have a carouse together, and then attend to business the next morning. But those days are over. Sales are made to-day by thinking, not drinking.

To-day every ambitious salesman must take care of his health. He must not be ill, nor half-ill, as so many people are.

Appearance counts for a great deal in a salesman. Intelligence counts for more; and both depend in the main upon good health.

I can call to mind a certain traveling salesman for a Chicago house — big, ruddy, smiling — the picture of health! He is welcome wherever he goes. Faces brighten in every room he enters. He has half won his battle before he begins to fight.

Perfect health makes a man almost irresistible. It makes him sway other men as a strong wind sways the branches of the tree.

Good health and good spirits, both! A salesman must be an optimist. It is a large part of his duty to put pluck into timid people — to buck up customers who are faint-hearted.

His head must be clear — as clear as a bell; and his heart must be light — as light as a child's, if he wishes to reach the 100 per cent. mark as a traveling salesman.

He must not be a worrier. He must be vaccinated against worries, else he will not last long on the road.

No other man, in any line of trade, or in any profession, has as many worries as a traveling salesman. He has 3 varieties:

1. PERSONAL WORRIES — created by his own habits, misfortunes or mistakes.

2. BUSINESS WORRIES — created by his company and his customers.

3. HOME WORRIES — created by his wife and children.

As you can see, he has a-plenty. Yet he must carry on — carefree, as though he hadn't a trouble in the world.

That is something that many a Sales Manager, and many a wife, does not think of — the way that worries handicap a traveler and knock his sales down.

If I were the wife of a traveler, I would write him a joyous letter every week —always to reach him on a Thursday, when he is beginning to feel the weight of his job. It would put his sales up 10 per cent. Few wives think of that.

A traveler must keep in fighting trim every week-day, until 6 P. M., anyway. If he wants to over-eat, or over-drink or over-smoke, he should do it after 6 P. M. or on Sunday.

Too much food, drink or tobacco, will slow a man up. It will take the snap out of him. Every athlete knows that, but few salesmen do.

In sport, men know the importance of keeping fit. Ask a jockey. Ask a pugilist. Better still, ask a trainer of athletes and he will tell you that it is no easy matter to keep in the pink of condition.

The wrong sort of a meal may make a jockey lose a race or a pugilist lose a fight.

Often the result of a race or a fight depends upon a fine point of fitness; and so does the result of many an interview, when a salesman is trying to sell goods.

A salesman, in fact, is more of a sportsman than an ordinary man of business. His job is really a game — just as much a game as base-ball is.

A sales interview is a battle of wits. It is brain against brain. The better man wins, if conditions are at all normal.

There is no routine work in a salesman's job — that is the big fact to remember.

It is all creative work — combative work, at times. No two customers are alike. A simple parrot-like talk will not do.

The traveling salesman who becomes me-chanical ceases to be a salesman. He becomes a mere carrier of samples — quite a different thing.

A traveling salesman has no control over his customers except mental control. He is entirely at the mercy of the customer. He is, in fact, a trespasser if the customer does not wish to see him.

The success of a traveling salesman, as you can see, is largely a matter of personality and intelligence.

A 100 per cent. salesman would be almost a human dynamo. He would be fit — ready in a flash to make good use of anything that happened to him.

A quick answer! How much depends on that in selling goods?

An opportunity that is snapped up in a second! That is the main secret of many a man's success.

Every day is a new day, to a traveling salesman. Every interview is a new adventure. He can no more afford to be careless than a lion-hunter can.

Many a time the result of a sales interview

is decided by the question of sheer vitality. The one that tires first, loses. The sticker wins.

I once knew a keen old business man, who piled up a $30,000,000 fortune; and he would never see anyone on an important business matter unless he was in good form.

"I always drink a cup of coffee," he said, "before I have an important interview with a buyer or a seller. I find it pays me to have my brain as keen as it can be, and not half asleep."

Every traveling salesman would do well to train his mind to notice — to compare — to remember — to create.

There are now plenty of cheap books that will help him to put an edge on his brain. He can develop his memory, too, up to a point.

He can store his mind with all manner of facts, as every sort of fact comes in useful to a salesman.

Customers have hobbies — all sorts of hobbies. One man is keen on music. Another is a lover of birds. Another follows the races. Another was a famous ballplayer in his youth.

If you can meet a man on his hobby you will go far towards securing his permanent good-will.

Selling, from first to last, is a mental process.

So, it is evident that the salesman's brain must not be dull and slow and deadened by narcotics.

It must be tuned up to concert pitch. Or, rather, to change the metaphor, his brain ought to be as quick as a pianist's fingers.

" If I stop practicing for a day," says Paderewski, " I notice it. If I stop for a week, my friends notice it. If I stop for a month, everybody notices it."

That is a great pianist's idea of keeping fit and that is the ideal that I would hold up to every ambitious salesman who wants to make the most of this life.

Keep fit. Keep fit or go into some other vocation that calls for less ability and self-control.

Every day of a traveling salesman's life is a

struggle of personalities. If he is inferior, he loses; if he is superior, he wins. That is the truth, in spite of a hundred sophistries and excuses.

KEEP FIT.

XI

HAVE A STOUT HEART

Chapter XI

HAVE A STOUT HEART

Be a Bit Of a Philosopher — Buck Up Your Customers — A Tip to Wives and Sales Managers

IF a traveling salesman's heart is not stout, it will very soon be broken — that's a truth that every company should bear in mind.

Many a salesman suffers a daily martyrdom for the reason that he has not strengthened himself for his job.

He perseveres, but he shortens his life. He becomes an old man at fifty.

Often, a heartbroken salesman keeps on with his work and trudges about as a mere order-taker. He is no longer a salesman. He is only a spiritless bag-carrier, who walks from door to door and says: " Nothing for me to-day, I suppose?"

The undeniable fact is that a salesman's job is a very lonely and depressing one, unless he takes himself in hand and uses a great deal of self control.

Many salesmen are temperamental. When they are at the top of their form, they could sell the Ten Commandments to a thief; but when they are down and depressed, they couldn't sell fried fish on a Friday.

Ups and downs! Hill-tops and valleys! And the daily average sale, at the end of the year, is very likely surprisingly small.

As anyone can see by a glance in the lobby of any hotel in an evening, many salesmen are in a Slough of Despond. They are bogged. They are discouraged. They are stuck.

This is natural enough. It springs out of the very nature of a salesman's job.

He is away from home for weeks at a stretch He is buffeted about on trains and in hotels.

He is a Robinson Crusoe. He has no co-workers. He is among strangers from Monday morning until Saturday noon.

All the complaints aimed at his company

fall upon him. He does not sit in an office and answer complaints by letter. No such luck. He must go and meet the angry complainer face to face.

He is out on the firing line, not back at the base.

He knows nothing of the pleasures of team-play. He is a lone hunter.

He is constantly facing an indifferent or unfriendly public, and pushing himself in where he is not invited.

He does his work without co-operation from anyone —without sympathy — without applause — often without a word of praise, even when he has done well.

Consequently, almost all salesmen have, at times, fits of depression. Every now and then they are down in the Pit. That is why it is absolutely necessary for every salesman to have a stout heart.

No one can face a dozen rebuffs in a day and keep smiling, unless he is stout-hearted.

These rebuffs do not all come from the customers, either. Some of them come from the home office, and some of them come from his wife.

Letters may make or break a man, so far as his day's work is concerned — home letters especially.

Grumbling, peevish, worrying letter! " You care more for your old firm than you do for me! " " You never think how lonely I am! " " You're having a gay time, while I'm cooped up at home! " And so on.

Pages of self-pity and pathos and petulance! And then the poor chap who gets one of these letters has to go out and face a world of strangers with a cheery smile.

How few wives of travelers realize that the one greatest asset of a salesman is CHEERFUL-NESS.

The letter that gives a salesman a heartache breaks him down as a salesman. Why don't wives realize that?

To the wives who read this, I would say: " If you are married to a traveling salesman, for Heaven's sake BUCK HIM UP. He has troubles you know nothing about, and unless you cheer him along, HE'LL FAIL and you will be the cause of it. KEEP THE HOME LIGHTS BURNING."

I know one wise salesman who never opens his letters until after lunch. By that time he has had a good start and done half-a-day's work. A man is not as vulnerable, he says, after lunch as he is at breakfast.

There are some Sales Managers who wear spurs. They prick and worry their salesmen. And salesmen have to put up with it, unless it is intolerable. It is a part of the job.

Managers and wives both are apt to forget that a salesman must not have the heart taken out of him, else he cannot sell goods.

A salesman works as he feels, usually. Therefore, he needs praise and encouragement more than anyone else in the company.

He needs cheery letters and good news and a jolly big banquet once a year, with the president of the company in the chair.

Also, he needs to pay attention to his own personal habits, as these often cause fits of depression.

He must not have a sluggish liver and he must have plenty of sleep. He must not lie half awake at night, else he will be half asleep in the daytime.

He must pull himself up if he finds that he is becoming morbid or pessimistic. A Dean or a Professor may be gloomy, but not a salesman.

Timidity, too, is a defect that must be overcome. It is a disastrous drawback, as many a young salesman discovers in his first year on the road.

A rebuff makes him lose his self-confidence for a time. His mind is filled with such thoughts as these:

" I'll leave this man until my next trip — it's too near lunch-time."

" This place is too busy — I'd better not bother them," etc.

All this is a sign of timidity, and no salesman can afford to be timid.

Many a time, in my younger days, I have walked up and down past a door before I had the courage to go in. But that was sheer weakness and nothing else. It had to be overcome.

A salesman cannot be thin-skinned. He must not take offence easily. He must not be a fragile flower.

Once an Irishman was killed at a Kilkenny Fair by a blow on the head. At the trial, it was proved that he had a very thin skull — a " paper skull," as it is called.

The prisoner, in self-defence, said to the Judge: " I put it to your Honor — what right had a man, with a skull like that, to go to the Kilkenny Fair? " The prisoner was acquitted.

So, if a salesman has a thin skin or a thin skull, he has no right to be in the Kilkenny Fair of traveling salesmanship. He is too perishable for such a strenuous profession. He should apply for a gentler job.

A salesman must be a good loser. He must be able to take punishment. In the course of a year, even the ablest salesman will, very likely, take more rebuffs than orders.

That is why a salesman must be a good sportsman. That is why he must take his job as a game, and not as a drudgery.

Win or lose, he must keep on playing. He must not let his company down. I have seen a salesman come into the hotel, as cheerful as a kitten and as bold as a lion, after a day of bad luck. He was a thoroughbred. No squealing. No fainting fits. No glooms. No despair.

The point to remember is that a salesman must carry enough cheerfulness for two — his customer and himself.

Cheerfulness is part of his ammunition — part of his equipment. He needs it as much as he needs his samples.

He must buck up his customers. Many of them are looking at Balance Sheets that would depress anybody. They need to be cheered up.

" My word, Jones, you're like a tonic," said a merchant to a salesman. You may be sure that Jones received an order.

So, a traveler needs to be stout-hearted to sell goods to discouraged dealers. He must have the spirit of Bernhardt.

Her motto was: " In spite of everything." In spite of age — in spite of troubles — in spite of a wooden leg, that indomitable French actress lived her life out to the last second at full speed.

She never slowed down — no, not even for Death. She went — crash — through the barrier.

A fully ripened and matured salesman is always a bit of a philosopher. His nature has grown too large to be troubled by trifles.

He is self-sufficient. He is not like a yacht — blown by the wind. Rather, he is like a liner. He goes forward, wind or no wind, because he carries his own power within him.

As you may have noticed, a young traveling salesman is very much like a peg-top. He must be made to go. Some run for a day and drop and some run for a week. They have to be continually driven forward.

The mature salesman is not like this. He does not become exhausted. He is not a peg-top nor a toy man who has to be wound up once a week.

In a word, he has " guts." He sticks. He takes his job as a daily adventure that is far to be preferred to any safe, stay-at-home, routine job.

Whatever else his job is, it isn't monotonous, thank God. There are never two days alike. And just when he thinks he knows all the bumps, he is apt to find a new one.

Then, at the end of his life — when his last journey has been made and his last order has been taken, he will have a deep satisfaction from his own stoutheartedness. He will say with Henley — " I thank whatever gods there be for my unconquerable soul."

XII

CREATE WELCOMES FOR YOURSELF

Chapter XII

CREATE WELCOMES FOR YOURSELF

Turn Your Customers Into Friends — Keep Your Selling On a Personal Basis

EVERY sales interview should begin and end on a personal note. The customer and the salesman should begin and end as MEN, not as buyer and seller.

This is courtesy and more than courtesy. It is a very important principle of salesmanship that there should be a pleasant finale.

Many salesmen seem to freeze suddenly as soon as the customer stops buying. They begin to think of the next customer or the next train.

Their eyes become dead and their manner becomes formal. Apparently, they seem to be saying to themselves:

" No more orders out of this fellow. Now for the next ordeal."

There may be a formal handshake and a polite good-bye, but if you have suddenly lost interest in people, you may be sure that they are keenly aware of it. They are seldom fooled by formalities. Every woman knows in a flash if your cordialty is real or make-believe; and many men do.

A salesman must always think of his next visit and prepare the way for it. If he does not do this, his visit may have done more harm than good.

He is a welcome-maker. He is an ambassador. His purpose is to create an *Entente Cordiale* between his company and his customer.

A welcome is very important. It saves time, for one thing. It gives the sales interview a running start; and it makes selling easy.

So, whenever a salesman fails to sell, his aim should be to create a welcome, at any rate, so that he will sell goods on his next visit.

Here you can see the reason, too, why a

salesman must not oversell or deceive a customer. If he does, he destroys his welcome.

There are plenty of welcome-killers floating about who call themselves traveling salesmen.

They drift from one employer to another, never remaining long anywhere; and what they cost a firm, no one can tell. But it would be cheaper, usually, to pay such men $100 a week to remain at home rather than to let them run amuck among customers.

All experienced and competent salesmen know that a large part of their work is to create and maintain cordial relations between their company and its customers, as well as to sell goods.

This is so vital a matter that a skilled salesman, when he is working a new territory, will concentrate all his attention upon the creation of welcomes, if his firm will allow him to do so.

A salesman, in a word, must be personally likeable. He must be congenial. If the customer comes to regard him as a pal, all is well.

A certain concern has a Sales Manager who worked up from being a traveling salesman.

He has for years been my ideal of a welcome-maker. He is the sort of man whom you would like to have as a next-door neighbor. His geniality is so sincere that it charms you.

Magnetism? Perhaps. Love for other people — more likely. This attractiveness or congeniality — whatever we may call it — is one of the most valuable attributes that a salesman can possess.

It is a curious fact that few technical men — chemists, engineers, specialists — possess this power of attracting people. That is why they so seldom succeed as salesmen.

They rely wholly upon facts and figures and technical knowledge. They ignore or despise feelings. They are seldom companionable. That is why, if I were selling engines, I would not select engineers as salesmen, but rather men who are skilled in salesmanship.

First and foremost, salesmanship means handling men, not machines. It means winning men over to the point of view of buying your goods.

Few technical men can understand this.

They treat all customers alike; and they have an underlying contempt, which some of them do not conceal, for the ignorance of their customer.

The fact is that a salesman's best asset is the goodwill of his customers. In this matter he is just like a company. I dare say that the goodwill of the Cunard Company, for instance, is worth more than a dozen of its best ships.

The goodwill of the Bank of England — what an enormous amount of money this must be worth! It is almost beyond anyone's power to tell exactly how much this would be.

So it is with the salesman. If he has built up a reputation for honesty, courtesy, knowledge of his goods, reliability, and so forth, he has acquired a real personal capital. Best of all, no one can take this from him. No thief can run away with it. No One Can Destroy It But Himself.

" Glad to see you again. I was just expecting you. Come along in." That is the sort of welcome that stamps a salesman as being a professional and not an amateur.

How many welcomes did he make last year? Is that not one of the best tests of his efficiency?

How few customers did he lose? What was his net gain in customers?

Can he say: " What I have, I hold "? Has he kept all his welcomes in good order, and has he added to the number?

Isn't it true that every skilled traveling salesman, as he reaches the end of his life, always measures his success by the number and quality of his friends?

Isn't it true that the measure of every man's success is the number of honest people who respect him and believe in him?

MAKE FRIENDS — that is the secret of good management and good salesmanship both.

MAKE FRIENDS — that is how to make any business succeed. Help other people, especially when they are in danger or in trouble.

Don't look on your customers as an orchard of apple trees or as a hive of bees. Don't regard them as the owners of something that you want.

Rather, look on other men as your pals and partners — as the friends who make your business pleasant as well as profitable.

MAKE FRIENDS AND YOUR SALES WILL TAKE CARE OF THEMSELVES. CREATE WELCOMES, AND YOU WILL NEVER LACK ORDERS.

The aim of every company is permanent patrons, not people who buy once and never again. The first sale to a man is seldom profitable. It is his continued patronage that counts.

New customers are costly. They have to be found either by advertising or by canvassing.

Moreover, an established concern is not like a street peddler, who sells continually to new people. A peddler can sell trash. He usually does. That is why he is obliged to keep moving.

But an established concern sells itself with its goods. It will be in the same place to-morrow — next year — in 40 years. It sells to you and your children and your children's children.

A big corporation does not consider the profit on every sale as much as it considers the permanence of its customers.

It regards its customers as its real capital. A customer who buys $2,500 worth of goods a year, for instance, is worth at least $5,000. Why? Because the net profit on $2,500 is about $250, which is the interest at 5 per cent. on $5,000.

To lose such a customer is precisely the same as losing $5,000 out of the bank — how few salesmen realize that?

That is why a salesman must always remember to create a welcome for his next visit. He must make sure that he has not done anything to push the customer away from his company.

All big corporations tend to become bureaucracies. This is bad enough in a factory, and it is fatal to a selling staff.

Traveling salesmen must never become mechanical. If they do, they cease to be profitable. Sales letters can be used instead and boxes of samples can be sent to dealers. If nothing is to be done except to show samples, and take orders, there are cheaper ways than by employing salesmen.

The selling of goods must always be kept on a personal basis, no matter how large the company is.

As soon as a customer feels that a manufacturer or wholesaler cares nothing for him he is apt to cut loose and buy elsewhere.

Customers refuse to be turned into numbers and handled like things. Almost all large firms forget this fact of human nature.

A one-man business, handled in a personal way, can always make more profits than a big amalgamation, where there is nothing but system and routine.

Andrew Carnegie, for instance, who treated all his customers as personal friends, made 40 per cent. dividends, while the big Steel Corporation has never made as much, not even in its best year.

People must be treated as people — that is

the last word on the subject. Customers above all! This is the apex of salesmanship.

Every true salesman makes a hobby of people. He studies human nature — the most fascinating subject in the world.

He has no hostility in his heart towards customers. He loves his fellow-beings. He keeps in touch with children and with old people as well. The whole octave of human nature — the whole range of feelings and thoughts and actions — are the constant delight of a salesman who has mastered the complete art of salesmanship.

THE HUMAN TOUCH! That is above all else. All trade and commerce, in the last analysis, is a matter of man to man. Keep human, and you will always have a welcome. And the man who is welcomed is the man who will win, in any of the rivalries of business.

CPSIA information can be obtained
at www.ICGtesting.com
Printed in the USA
LVHW061521210123
737528LV00028B/1185